PSYCHIC EMPATH

An Essential And Practical Guide To Psychic
Development ,Releasing Anxiety And A Sens
Of Self

JUDITH HEAL

Table of Contents

Introduction

Without empathy, people would go about their lives without considering the feelings and thoughts of other people. Every person has differing perspectives on life; therefore, if we did not have something that made us accommodate each other, life would be very complicated. We all experience moods, joy, sadness, pain hurt et cetera, and if we focus only on the things happening in our lives, we will limit our capabilities. It is easy to jump into conclusions if we do not take a moment to truly understand what the other people stand for. Lack of empathy normally leads to bad feelings, misunderstandings, poor morale, conflict, and even divorce.

When one uses empathy in real life to understand why a person is angry, or a child is throwing a tantrum, he/she might learn about things in their lives that trigger the behavior. For example, one might find that something happened at home, thus pushing the angry person to act out or that the child did not have a meal in the morning thus they are not okay.

Empathy enables one to ask questions about the situation or behavior of another person before taking a defensive stance or reacting to some emotions. There may still be the need for disciplinary action, but one should use empathy first. Empathy makes a person feel valued and understood even if they are punished for the wrong deeds, and as such, they will accept responsibility for their action. Empathy is currently the missing link in schools, families, workplaces, and the world at large.

There are a few misunderstandings that arise when one is applying empathy in real life. Some people believe that being empathetic involves agreeing with the opinion of everybody else. That is wrong and will only lead to exhaustion. Understand the perceptions of the other person, acknowledge them but you do not have to sing along every tune.

Other people believe that being empathetic involves doing what everyone else wants or doing anything to make others happy. That is wrong. You are not obligated to please everyone; you do not have to cooperate in every other situation. Just because you fail to accommodate every other matter does not mean that you are evil. The world is complicated; therefore, use empathy but do not agree with everything.

Empathy does not mean being there for someone for a lifetime. After listening to a person and offering a solution, you do not have to always be there for them, you have other tasks to accomplish and if you feel that the person is just using you, walk away. Empathy does not mean you should have no ego or intention. Once you assist someone, allow your ego to help you walk away or change the discussion.

Applying empathy in real life can be challenging therefore, there are investments that one needs to make, and they include time, patience and proactivity.

1.   Time

It takes some time for one to listen to others, pay attention and not jump into conclusions. Coming up with good solutions also takes time. In most cases, we want to arrive at an answer very first without taking the time to understand; this only leads to more problems. Empathy is like watching sand draining in an hourglass; it takes time, but not that much time, and it is very satisfying.

2.   Patience

Empathy does not only take time; it requires a lot of patience. Paying attention to someone, listening to everything they are saying, and selecting a comprehensive solution takes a lot more than just jumping into conclusions, listing arguments and repeating an opinion. Normally people fail to give the patience and attention required when making conversations; therefore, it becomes harder than it should be.

3.   It takes proactivity

Some people think that empathy should only be given when both parties have something to gain. In the real sense, we should show empathy even to people who show no sign of understanding our perspectives and opinions. This can be very frustrating, and one might find it very unfair, but empathy begins with you. It will not work if both of you wait on each other to start the conversation.

4.   Be the role model, set the example, be a good listener and do not talk until the other person is done. Understand the opinions of other people but remember you do not have to agree with them. Being empathetic can be a tough challenge but still, there are many people that practice it. Apply empathy every day and enjoy the benefits.

Of all of the talents an Empath possesses, listening may be one of the most notable. Listening skills are effective in any situation and are what help us to engage more fully with the world around us. When you can hear what is going on, you can participate more closely and provide a keener sense of understanding. You can also hear things on another level- things that are unspoken but nevertheless still communicating to us through body language, gestures, facial expressions, and energy.

For the Empath, listening comes naturally and so does absorbing energy from the person you are talking to. This can mean that you end up taking on a lot of negativity, anger, frustration, and other uncomfortable emotions. As you start to feel the effects of these feelings, it can make it harder to listen well and comfortably. The ability to listen can get upset by the emotional energy of the people around you and can distort your emotional state as well.

Finding your tactics for listening from the heart can be helpful, and with a little practice, you can learn how to compliment being a heartfelt listener while still protecting and shielding your energy from being disrupted from the negativity involved. As an Empath myself, I have tried a variety of techniques and models to help me find the best

Ch1. How to Recover Positive Energies by Handling Negative Influence

When lots of people hear about the phrase negative influence, they assume it has to do with drugs, alcohol, or other social vices. However, the phrase negative influence is more than social vices. Negative influence implies those bad influences that push you into making bad decisions. For example, you can be influenced into thinking bad about yourself. This will lead to low self-esteem. You can also be affected to think a negative thought about your life or your job. This could lead to suicide if not curtailed fast. Negative influence doesn't stop at having negative thoughts or suggestions; it can lead to negative habits as well.

Getting rid of removing negative influence can be a daunting challenge. Your task removing negative influence can be made more difficult if people with negative habits surround you.

Furthermore, these individuals will remind you of your negative habits and forced to indulge in them even when you are trying to remove them. However, all hope is not lost. All you need is commitment and perseverance, and you will be able to remove negative influence, turn things around and begin to leave your life with more positivity.

Display a Positive Attitude with a Negative Person

However, to handle or diffuse their negativity, you should show them a positive response when they show their negative attitude. Recover your positive attitude by balancing out their negative displays with your positive one.

For example, when your negative friend says that no one cares about you, say that your friends or family love you very much. If they make a bad comment about something or someone, counter their statement by saying how vital the thing is or how generous the individual they tried to put down is. Canceling they negative words with your positive response will nullify their negative influence on you and address their negativity openly and proactively.

Stop Negative Talk/ Thought About Yourself

Negative self-talk is as damaging as negative habits. You can engage in negative talk but only focusing on the bad things happening in your life rather than the good ones. Negative talk can also apply to the way you think about yourself. For example, a night of hangout may be canceled by your pals. Rather than letting it go, you begin to tell yourself that it was canceled because of you. You use words like 'no one likes me that is why they don't want to hang out with me'. Another example can be something like this. After having a very productive day at work, you come home rather than being happy about your day; you begin to tell yourself how much work you couldn't get done.

Furthermore, negative talk means that you have a narrow-minded view of the world around you. When things are not working out for you and every turn, so there is no possible positive outcome in sight, which means that you have a feeling of imminent disaster coming your way.

If you engage in this type of talk about yourself, it is time you put an end to it, or you won't remove negative influence from your family and life.

Turn Negative Talk to Positive Ones

If you want to remove negative influence, you need to turn negative talk about yourself to positive ones. The power of the mind is crucial to the way you see yourself. Negative thoughts lead to negative speech, and negative talk leads to negative influence. You can change all that but having positive thoughts about yourself and, in turn, have a positive talk about yourself.

Start by evaluating any negative thought that comes into your mind. After evaluation, give a positive response to that particular negative thought. Make use of positive responses like ' I can do better than I did yesterday.' Make use of the ' can and will' phrase to dispel any negative thought that comes to your mind. Remember, you are what you think of yourself.

Change must come from within before it can manifest outwards. Start your day every day with a positive affirmation of yourself. With consistency in your part, you will remove negative influence in no time from every area of your life.

Be Yourself

It's easy to impress someone or look good for someone, but it's not always wise. The simple fact is you can't always satisfy everyone. Instead of making yourself look good for others, why not focus on making yourself happy? Don't to impress anyone, let alone a negative person. Be yourself and spend quality time trying to figure out the things that make you happy. Spend time with people that will accept who you are and what you stand for. Don't pursue the wrong thing.

Determine Your Attitude

A person associating with a negative person does so at his/her own peril. They are toxic and introduce toxicity into your life. You don't have the will power to make your own decisions because you are surrounded by pessimists.

Don't allow negative people to dictate how you should respond or how your mood should be. You are yourself and in control of whatever that's happening to you. Choose how you want to behave. Choose how you want to be. Decide how you run your life because it's yours and no one else's.

Negative people can bring out the worst in you. It's quite normal. What's more important is how you let this negativity control you. Do not let your emotions get the better part of you. Determine your state of reaction. If you find yourself in negative situations, learn to control your emotions.

Reduce Negative Habits

You can't get rid of or remove negative influence if you don't remove negative habits first. These negative habits, like smoking, heavy drinking, and regular partying, could make you feel good momentarily, but they have a lasting negative impact on your dreams and aspirations. They generally leave you with a wicked hangover and a negative feeling in the morning.

This negative feeling in the morning will cause time mismanagement.

Time mismanagement means that you won't have enough time during the day to pursue your dreams and engage in those activities that will facilitate your career development.

Stopping all your negative habits will be a good way to handle negative influences in your life. Still, from experience, I know it will be difficult to stop all bad habits suddenly, so I suggest cutting back on your negative habits. This will go a long way to removing negative influence in your life. For example, rather than go out every night after work to the bar for a couple of drinks that usually lead to one too many, cut it back to once or twice a week.

Some people give the excuse of being stressed as the reason they drink every night. You can handle your stress by engaging in healthy activities like evening runs around your neighborhood. If you're not fond of running, you can get a bicycle and cycle around your neighborhood as well. You will feel less stressed after engaging in any of these activities. You might as well have friends over once or twice a week and cook for them. Social interaction is one good way to get rid of stress.

Have a Positive Lifestyle

You can get rid of negative influence by leaving a positive lifestyle. You can start by having healthy meals. Healthy meals should include a large portion of self-made meals and less junk. A balanced diet of protein, vegetables, and fruits, as well as milk, should be part of your meals. Remember to drink adequate water as well to stay hydrated. Cut down or soda or possibly avoid it completely as well as other sugary drinks.

The next part of your positive lifestyle should be to get sufficient sleep. This is one thing most people don't pay much attention to but, a sufficient amount of sleep every day plays a role in your mood and how you feel about yourself. When you get a sufficient amount of sleep, you won't get exhausted before the day even begin and you will be in a good mood. In the current economy, it is easy for you to neglect sleep, but it is essential you sleep at a fixed time to ensure you don't deviate from it. Set up your bedroom to ensure you get as much sleep as possible. If you maintain your sleep schedule, you will find yourself more relaxed and in a better positive frame of mind.

Furthermore, the recommended time for adequate sleep is nine hours, ensure you get up that number in a day.

Take Note of Your Unhealthy Habits

It is normal for an individual to have some unhealthy habits so you shouldn't feel that you are the only one with them. However, knowing what your bad habits are and looking for ways to eliminate them will assist you to remove negative influence.

To effectively take note of these bad or negative habits, think about habits that make you feel depressed and sad about yourself. Those habits that leave you with the feeling that your life sucks and drains your energy making it difficult for you to focus on doing things that will aid your development and influence your life positively.

The obvious examples of these habits are heavy doses of alcohol consumption, substance abuse, heavy partying and unhealthy eating habits. The less obvious ones are unhealthy relationships that leave you with senses of depression and sadness. Another example of this type of habit is self-esteem hate and loathing, low self-esteem. It's highly recommended that you document these bad or negative habits so you can know how to handle them.

Ch2.Quiz to Assess Your Degree of Empathy

Read the statements below to yourself and keep a careful note of how many of them you agree with. Use a piece of paper and pen to tally the number of times you identify with the statements--this number will be your empathic score. If you agree strongly and frequently with a statement, mark down 2 points. If you agree somewhat, occasionally, or under specific circumstances, mark down 1 point for yourself. If you do not identify or agree with a statement at all, mark down 0 points.

Try to be as honest with yourself as possible. Answer with your gut, and don't overthink your responses. Also, remember that this self-assessment is designed to evaluate your current empathic abilities, which are fluid and in constant fluctuation. If you find you are torn on any statements, perhaps because you once identified strongly with them but now you no longer do, or vice versa, choose whatever answer resonates most powerfully with your present-day self.

It might be best to take this quiz when you are alone, calm, and able to focus, attending to no one else's needs but your own. If you are indeed an empath, your answers may be impacted by the feelings, judgments, or values of others around you, which can ultimately skew your scoring results.

1.   I feel emotions more deeply than most.

2.   I have been called "very sensitive," or perhaps even "too sensitive," by others.

3.   I can become overwhelmed or uncomfortable in large crowds.

4.   I sometimes feel the need for complete, uninterrupted solitude (maybe with quiet and or darkness, but not sleep) to gather my thoughts or "recharge" my energy.

5.   I can tell when people are lying or trying to mask their feelings, even if no one else around seems to see it.

6.   I am very conscious of how my actions will affect those around me.

7. I find the emotional reactions of other people-- laughing, crying, scowling in anger-- be genuinely contagious, regardless of the emotional state I bring to the interaction; even if I am over-the-moon with personal joy, I can be quickly moved to tears by someone else's sorrow.

8. I am deeply bothered by situations of injustice, and often can't help but try to find a solution or remedy, even if it's none of my business or beyond my reach to do so.

9. I am drawn to animals, and I am more comfortable with them than in the company of some humans.

10. I am often told that I am a great listener.

11. I tend to take care of others before I address my own needs.

12. My emotional reactions seem to last longer than they do for other people--it might take me days or weeks to get over something that other people move on from in a matter of hours.

13. In a phone call (or another form of communication where I can't see someone's face) I can read someone's emotional state just from the sound of their voice, and usually gather this from only one or two words of greeting.

14. There are certain forms of graphic media that I just can't stomach--violence, for instance, or humiliation-based comedy is almost painful for me to watch, and I find it hard to shake the feeling off even after it's over.

15. People often open up to me, even those I don't know very well, sharing secrets, confessions, or other pieces of intimate knowledge.

16. I often find myself getting emotionally involved in other people's problems or successes; I might be deeply distraught over a friend's break-up or thrilled when a colleague receives a well-deserved promotion.

17. I frequently catch myself mirroring the body language of others, or mimicking accents and patterns of speech, during conversations.

18.   I am more sensitive than most to temperature, and usually, feel chilly in places where others are perfectly comfortable.

19.   I can't help reading between the lines or hearing the subtext of a conversation just as loudly as what is articulated verbally.

20.   My emotions tend to resonate throughout my entire body; I have a hard time compartmentalizing or ignoring them.

21.   I sometimes experience synesthesia, where two or more of my sensory perceptions are intertwined (a sensation of feeling color, perhaps, or seeing sounds, associating numerical values with musical notes, or feeling that certain days or months are linked to locations or emotional states, etcetera.)

22.   I can be easily distracted by an external stimulus.

23.   Anything that feels inauthentic--a book or movie, a business, or even someone's personality--is a huge turnoff for me, and I cannot stand to be

around such things for more than a few minutes without experiencing pain or discomfort.

24. I do not mind being alone if I can determine how I send the time; I might prefer to stay home on Saturday night to read or paint or cook, rather than attend a party.

25. I am susceptible to bright lights, odors, and sounds, sometimes profoundly bothered by them while others can easily ignore them.

26. When conflict arises between people, I know but does not involve me, I still feel hurt, angry, confused or sad, and I am preoccupied until I've taken action to encourage peacemaking.

27. Miscommunication is profoundly frustrating for me to experience or witness, even between strangers.

28. I can sometimes experience two or more contrasting emotions simultaneously; I might be full of joy and fear and sadness, feeling each emotion equally and all at once.

29. I feel deeply connected to underdogs, both in entertainment media and in real life. I can be protective of friends and total strangers alike-- anyone who seems especially vulnerable to victimization.

30. I have trouble accepting absolutes, believing that anyone is purely good or evil, that anything is decisively the best or the worst of its kind; I think the truth is always complex, multifaceted, and fluid, because it is largely a matter of perspective.

31. It is sometimes challenging for me to stay present at the moment; my mind is often stuck in the past or fixed in the future.

32. I react to most stimuli quickly and viscerally; I am not the type to sit back and wait to see how things play out before I decide how to feel about the situation.

33. Watching group interactions can be fascinating to me; I sometimes feel as if I can see or sense a complex web of emotions tying every member of the group together, like a game of cat's cradle,

influencing their movements, behaviors, and attitudes.

34. The planned trajectories of my days can be thrown off course by fairly small triggers. Something as small as a sharp exchange, a missed green light, a good sign or bad omen, even a momentary sense of deja vu, might cast a ripple effect on my itinerary for the rest of the day or even week.

35. Music, movies, books, dance, and other art forms often give me a sense of being entirely transported to a different time, place, and reality; or, they might trigger an out-of-body experience for me. They can deliver a feeling of transcendence, even if I have no reason to identify with them.

36. I have an eye for small details that others frequently overlook.

37. When I connect with someone I like, we often form an extraordinarily deep bond, and we do so very quickly.

38. Conversely, I often meet people and immediately get bad feelings about them without being able to explain why. That may even be the case if the person in question displays kindness towards me at a surface level, which makes me even more uncomfortable.

39. I don't usually dominate conversations or feel comfortable talking about myself for long periods. I tend to listen or ask questions to encourage input from everyone involved.

40. I have a talent for bringing shy children, adults, or animals, out of their shells.

Your score

Tally up all your zeroes, ones and twos to find your current position on the empathy quotient scale. Remember not to let these numbers discourage you or give you too big of a head--empathy is fluid, and there is always room for growth!

0-20 - Little to no empathic connection

If fewer than twenty of these questions resonated with you, don't interpret that to mean you are incapable of empathy. This score might indicate an empathy deficient condition or disorder, but it also could come from an individual with average, or even heightened, empathic abilities who have learned to close themselves off temporarily. People sometimes reject or turn away from empathic sensitivity as a response to being hurt, having their ego severely bruised, experiencing trauma or grief, as a reaction to long periods of solitude, or a lack of privacy and personal space. Whatever the reason for your score, try to view this number as a jumping off point to start building your empathic energy. Try this test again in a few months, and you may be pleasantly surprised by your growth.

20-40 - Average empathic sensitivity

You are sensitive to the world around you, but selectively. You have a healthy sense of self, you know what you like, and you understand your value system. You recognize the boundary between your own emotions and other people's feelings but can still empathize fully in appropriate situations.

At this position on the empathy quotient scale, your boundaries need to be strong. If you surround yourself with people who display low empathetic sensitivity levels, you may find your score gradually decreases under their influence.

40-80 - Heightened empathic ability

Your empathic capability is above average, but perhaps not so strong that you have been forced to reckon with it entirely. You've found it helpful in some ways, but profoundly confusing and frustrating at times, too. That can be a turbulent awakening experience, as empathetic sensations come to you seemingly from out of nowhere, unpredictably and often at extremely inconvenient times. If your sensitivity is awakened but not trained, you are vulnerable to the whims of the world, like a rowboat in the sea without a paddle. You'll first want to enhance your empathic sensitivity and understanding, and then determine the specifics of your empathic type, before ultimately learning how to balance and ground your energy.

80-120 - Advanced empathic power

This score could alternatively be called "severe empathic sensitivity," depending on how well you've managed your abilities thus far. You feel a great deal more empathy than most, which leaves you quite vulnerable to toxic energy, emotional contagion, and depletion. With education, training and spiritual guidance, you'll be able to manage your power and maintain your energy levels, but it will take plenty of focus, determination, and patience to reach a point of emotional stability. With this degree of power, your reach may very well exceed your grasp, so it's important to seek out experienced mentors, metaphysical healers, and spiritual teachers to help guide you to a place of deeper understanding.

Ch3.Practical Exercises for Empaths

Shutting yourself from others is incredibly harmful psychologically for anyone, not just for empaths. This increases the sensitivity we feel when around others. We want to be able to function at our best in all situations and not become overly sensitive to 'regular' people.

A method many sensitives use unconsciously to stop the constant bombardment of other emotions and energy, is to distract themselves. Distracting works to lessen the impact of external stimulus. But there are various negative forms of distraction such as alcohol, drugs, sex, porn and junk food which can lead to a reliance or an unhealthy addiction. Most of these addictions shift our perception into a state where we are not as aware, this allows us to escape feeling the pain in the world. Try to avoid these at all costs!

In this part, we will look at positive exercises and forms of distraction which will help support you no matter what you're faced with without relying on unhealthy vices.

Using Affirmations

Many people use affirmations nowadays, they have become incredibly popular in all walks of life. They're positive statements repeated over and over to help us escape negative thought patterns while promoting positive ones. They can help keep an empath strong particularly in an overwhelming situation. You can create your own affirmations if something in particular resonates with you. Here are a few of the ones which I have found helpful -

'I refuse to absorb other people's energy. I can acknowledge how others are feeling, but I now shield myself from absorbing anything from them'.

'I can allow others close to me, without taking on their energy or emotions'.

'I feel and connect with my own feelings before anyone else's'.

Do you struggle saying no to people? This is a common occurrence among sensitives, here is an idea which I found helpful when presented with something I wasn't sure about. If for example, a friend of colleague asks you out for drinks in the evening, instead of agreeing immediately, respond with 'Ok, I will just have to check my schedule and let you know' - This isn't saying no! But it is in fact giving you some breathing space to decide whether or not this is something you want to do. With this kind of response, you don't feel like you have been put on the spot and that you must respond immediately. This gives you time to process the request and hopefully muster up the courage within to say no (if you don't feel like doing what was requested). Beginning to honor your feelings is incredibly important.

Here are three unfinished sentences which you can work with to help build your sense of boundaries. Try to come up with as many different responses as you can. By doing this you are gradually beginning to reinforce and develop stronger boundaries.

1) I have the right to ask for.........

Some answer here could include - space, respect etc.

2) To have enough time and energy to function at my best, it is ok to..........

Examples - refuse invitations, do my own work first etc.

3) If I refuse others, they may......

Examples - not like me, talk badly about me, respect me more etc

Without talking care of your own boundaries, you are effectively hindering yourself from living a happy and successful life. That's what it comes down to. Over time, this becomes easier. Helping others at your own expenses is detrimental to the whole.

Exercise

Exercise is an absolute must. I have personally found it to be one of the main tools I use that helps me enjoy life as an empath. The right training will not only exercise the physical body but the nervous system also (the root of your sensitivity). By exercising to engage the nervous system, we can almost reset our minds and bodies. This is exactly how I feel after a workout, as though someone has pushed a button and I have been energetically reset. It works incredibly well to clear away negative or any stagnant energy. It also increases the flow of freshly oxygenated blood all around the body. These are just some of the many benefits associated to exercise.

Another important tip is to stay away from public mirrors. The ones you find in gyms and clothes shops. Empaths can pick up negative energies being reflected to them from mirrors especially if the people who have been looking at their reflections are egotistical or self-absorbed. The empath can often take on this negative energy as their own.

Clearing your energy to create healthier boundaries

Reduce negativity - Due to our sensitive nature, we pick up negativity very easily. To help overcome this, empaths should start distancing themselves from negativity as much as possible. This can include people you know, certain places, even the news and social platforms. The TV and social media can really impact the empath on a subconscious level, they may not realize it at the time but they are picking up a lot of negativity from these sources particularly from the news, world affairs, soap operas and even reality TV shows.

Balance - Living a balanced life, is important for anyone, none more so than for an empath. This includes all areas of life such as diet, work, health, sleep, exercise etc. Keeping all aspects in some kind of balance help avoid becoming over stimulated. Try not to overdo it, as you'll likely need longer to recover. I have personally found I can only exercise 2-3 times a week, any more than this and I tend to feel burnt out. Taking adequate rest is also important and will improve your overall health and well-being.

Determine what is not yours –

Sometimes we walk into a room or a situation and feel like we have energetically picked up a mood or a vibe which wasn't ours. Try to bring your conscious awareness to any feelings you suspect don't belong to you. If you don't feel it is yours then make a choice to discard it, send the unwanted energy away and down into the earth. This can be done easily, simply holding your focus and stating the intention in your mind while visualizing the emotion leaving you.

Declutter –

Since empaths fundamentally must claim ownership over their own energetic space and stop others intruding in it, they should also take the same care with their physical areas. If you are messy, untidy or have a lot of clutter, take the time to clear your physical space, doing this will clear your mind and energy also. Negativity tends to breed in clutter and mess.

Crystals for protection –

Crystals are a gift and a spiritual superpower for promoting self-care. Anything can be used as a symbol of protection whether that is a piece of jewelry or a crystal. The most important thing is that you believe in whatever you are trusting for your protection. This belief alone will help protect you. People find it easy to trust in crystals due to their natural Earthly healing properties and they're fairly inexpensive to buy. If you are interested in learning in depth knowledge on how to use crystals and how to get the most out of these powerful stones then please check out my other book - Crystal Healing: Heal Yourself & Transform Your Life.

Now we will take a look at some crystals which work incredibly well as protection for empaths and sensitives.

Rose Quartz

This is a great crystal for empaths to possess simply for its grounding properties. It is often referred to as the 'Love Stone', since is resonates and works to repair the heart chakra. These qualities give the user a boost while helping to keep others negative emotions out of their space. It promotes all types of love, such as self-love, romantic, unconditional and platonic. Since it is a quartz, this means it has a high energy that can help bring a positive loving vibration into almost all circumstances. By bringing more love into an empath's daily life, it helps to lower stress while carrying warmth to everyone who is present. It is also used to improve self-esteem and attract genuine love into our lives. All these positive qualities bring balance to the emotions while helping to reduce stress and anxieties.

Black Tourmaline

This has been referred to as the 'must have' crystal for empaths. Known for its protective qualities this crystal enables the carrier to shield and deflect away any negative or low vibrational energies. It does this by processing any bad energy which comes into the auric field whether it's from other people or the environment. It also acts as a filter to protect us, which only allows good energies in, such as love, joy and kindness.

When carried regularly it neutralizes and purifies our own negative thought patterns by filtering them into positive energy. It is renowned as an extremely effective grounding stone; it achieves this by creating a connection between the body and Earth. This contact helps to align and balance the energy centers (chakras) while channeling positive healing energy through the whole physical body.

Sugilite

This crystal comes in a striking violet color and resonates with the 7th chakra - the crown. It creates a firm impermeable bubble around the carrier which helps protect them from negative energies of the environment and unwanted thought forms from others. It's incredibly effective at preventing energetic attacks from energy vampires by dissolving the bad energy patterns headed our way. Its power enables the user to go through their daily activities with a sense of inner strength and grace. Due to its activation of the crown chakra, it helps bring healing light in from the head down to the 1st chakra - the root. This influx of positive energy promotes balance and well-being that keeps us strong when faced with negativity.

Lapis Lazuli

A very popular and attractive stone that has been used for many thousands of years, particularly prevalent with the ancient Egyptians. It is best known for its protective qualities and its ability to repair, seal and strengthen the auric field. This helps in dissolving any negative emotions or energies which have been picked up. Lapis is a crystal of truth which helps increase self-awareness within the empath, with this we become more conscious of what belongs to us and what doesn't. In the same way, it allows what doesn't belong to us to be released and 'brought to the surface'. Lapis works with the third eye chakra, which is the seat of perception, with this we are able to gain clarity and 'see' exactly what is occurring around us energetically. Although, empaths sense this, they do not always clearly understand what is happening. It also helps promote grounding and restores balance.

Ch4.Positive Affirmations to Be Made Daily

An affirmation is a positive sentence that will affect your conscious and subconscious mind. Repeating an affirmation has the power of helping it manifest. If you visualize and repeat your affirmation continuously, it will help in the manifestation of your desires much faster. Using affirmations will make the result more profound.

 Positivity plays a very important role in your life. People probably tell you to stay positive all the time while assuring you that everything will be fine. There is more to this than just words. Positive thoughts and energy can be very powerful. If you focus on the bad things and negative thoughts in your life, this will result in the manifestation of those.

Thinking and acting positively will therefore help in the manifestation of positive results in your life. I'm not saying that a miracle will happen and you will get an expensive car just by saying you will get it the next day; however, if that car is what you want, use it in your affirmation sentence. When you practice and repeat this affirmation over time, it will help you get that car. You may be wondering how this is possible. Well, when you focus on that car or just anything else, you know what you want.

meditation will help to change your mindset and life to a much more positive one. This will make it possible to be determined and work singularly until you achieve your goal of buying that car. This is how the manifestation will work in your favor. When you keep lamenting your bad luck or anything negative, your energy and thoughts are focused on those. This drains you of the positive energy required to live your life more productively. Can you understand a little now?

Negative thoughts can arise at any moment, and they may be very overwhelming at times; however, with the help of Empathy, you can exercise control over these thoughts and turn them into more positive ones. Your negative thoughts should never overpower the positivity in you. For this, you need to maintain balance in your chakras, lead a healthy lifestyle, and practice regularly.

Healing with Affirmations

Affirmations are an easy and simple tool for healing. There is no complicated formula, symbol, or technique involved. This is why it is one of the easiest tools to use in your daily life, but it has a profound impact.

One of the ways to heal with affirmations is to chant. Chanting is a practice that is used all over the world and in various religions. Just repeating certain words with complete faith has a way of harnessing power into them. This is why you should try repeating your affirmation like a chant whenever you get a chance.

Use the affirmation chant to charge a bottle of water or some crystal that you can carry with you all day. You can also write the affirmation on some paper and place a glass of water over it. This water can be consumed or sprayed around your space when it is charged with the affirmation.

Another method involves using Empath more proactively. Write your affirmation on a paper and then practice over it with your palms. You can either hold the affirmation paper or hover over it with your hands. You can also do this by keeping a bottle of water on the table. Now use your palms to hover over this bottle. the associated symbols as you chant the affirmation. Try visualizing the outcome of your affirmation while you move your hands over the water. This also helps to charge that bottle of water with positive energy, and you can continue consuming it throughout the day.

Meditating on an affirmation is a healthy and effective practice. Take time out every day to meditate over your desired goal. Sit in a peaceful place and take some calming breaths. Close your eyes and begin chanting the affirmation. Meditate on the outcome that you desire. Visualize it happening. This can be a powerful tool and will strengthen your belief in the possibility of the affirmation manifesting.

Using crystals is another great alternative to try. Find the appropriate crystal for your purpose and cleanse it before you use it. Crystals absorb energy from each person they come in contact with, and you need to make sure the crystal you use is cleansed for your purpose. Now hold the crystal in your palms and use to charge it. Focus and use your complete concentration to repeat your affirmation as you hold the crystal. Direct the affirmation into the crystal and manifest the energy from your third-eye chakra. Visualize a white light coming from your chakra and beaming into the crystal. Then imagine the outcome of your affirmation happening. Use this charged crystal and keep it in a sacred space. You can also choose to carry it with you at all times.

All of the ways given above are just some of the options available to you. You can heal with affirmations in many ways. The affirmation that you create in the first place should be a powerful and meaningful sentence.

Ch5.Avoiding the Negativity That Sometimes Plagues Empaths

The transference of energy from other people is a real challenge in today's world. Highly sensitive people are often plagued with this phenomenon and wonder what to do about it. Signals carrying the energy from those around us is often involuntary. It just happens. Sometimes we can gain from these encounters but most often, they are a weight that can drag us down and ruin a perfectly good day.

When we absorb other people's feelings and emotions, they become mixed up within our own similar inclinations and thoughts. When this happens, things can get a bit more involved and interrupt the natural flow of our own lives so that things don't get done or become halted altogether. For this reason, we must guard against the potential for misinterpretations of these bundles of feelings in order to have an actively progressive flow of our own information and forward motion.

When you find yourself in a room with a very negative individual, their "bad" energy can actually very quickly be activated in you. In order to prevent this from happening, the first step to take is to take a moment and look inwards, try to identify the true source of the negative energy. Is it you and was it always there inside you, or is it the other persons energy invading your otherwise happy system? In most cases, you will be able to learn that it is indeed not yours and was not present in your immediate feelings and emotions until that other person walked into the room. You must then take steps to let it go. Close your eyes and visualize who you are. Embolden yourself with the strength that you know you have always had within you and hold on tightly to that which you believe. Since you are a positive life form, this will manifest in those negative energies leaving your body and your mind. Remove yourself from surroundings containing negative thought patterns and feelings. Just walk away from it and do everything you can to avoid repeating this type of situation and condition in the future.

Another trait empath all exhibit is that they are all hyper-sensitive to the effect of their surroundings. When an empath is in a space where harmony abounds, they are most at home, as they will always mimic the happy and harmonious qualities of the room. Consequently, when they are in an environment where there is negative and dark energy, the opposite happens, and they must remove themselves as quickly as possible which is exactly what they usually do. Actually, this is something all normally energized people should also do. Nobody should have to put up with those who simply drag us down with their whiny grievances.

Here are some things that you can do in order to protect and embolden yourself from the negative and nonproductive energy of those around you:

•   Set your limits and boundaries. Negative people will recognize this in you and will generally move away from you.

•   Be selective in where you go, who you are willing to speak with and always be sure to be in control of you.

•   Don't get sidelined. Keep your antenna's up and use your special awareness to stay clear of others bad behavior and negative energies.

•   Stay positive. Don't let anyone or anything drag you down. It is much easier to stay positive within yourself than to have to battle your way back up after being dragged down unnecessarily.

•   Remember who you are and how much you love being you. You are above the fray when it comes to bad energy. Use your own "intact" systems to stay strong.

So if you've thought it over and wondered to yourself just how to stay positive when your find yourself in a negative environment; stick to the rules set out here and things will gradually begin to smooth out and become much easier for you. If these are people you just cannot avoid, and would really rather avoid, you must have a protection program in place, or you will suffer, and they will drag you down.

There is really no sense in letting this happen if your already know that it is a "given," with a certain person or set of people, that it has already previously been proven to be so. You can do this. Know the parameters, set up your own system in your mind when you know you must face them again, and keep it up!

You may want to think of in the abstract; be creative. Think of your next meeting with these low energy people as a heading. Think of the upcoming meeting, class, group, or whatever the case may be, as the heading on a part of a book. The heading tells the reader what is coming, and then the data pours out and is indeed, "as advertised." The heading predicted it because it knew for a fact what was coming next, and the data had to work closely with the heading because they work in tandem with each other. They are a team!

Now, breaking this theory down, you are the heading and the "people" in the group are the data. If your heading says, "Do not try to mess with me because I am protected, and it won't work!" They will take one look at you and immediately back off. Problem solved.

As stated, toxic people, whether they are consciously aware of it or not, do not do well with boundaries or "rules of engagement." These would be "your" rules, so you are in charge. When going into battle, be armed and dangerous. Be ready for the enemy.

I know that sounds a bit terse but it gets the point across and the alternative is having to set through hours of soul destroying and painful negativity that you know within yourself that you don't like and you don't need. Just do your homework and take control. It will be easy once you understand how to do it.

And there is more; again, why you know that you must see them, be with them, and interact with them, keep it short and concise so that there is no room for "small talk" or any unnecessary banter. Keep the communications brief and keep the material light whenever possible. Remember, toxic people will search for key areas in your speaking on which to pounce. This will create a scenario where they look better. This is their MO. If the conversation is by telephone, set a timer so you have control.

Weigh out the consequences of new topics that may arise in conversation and know which are worth dealing with and which are worth tossing into the circular file as soon as possible. Observe others intention in their speaking. Where are they attempting to take the conversation?

You really do need to protect yourself from what could be called "secondhand stress." Just being around people who operate out of drama can be very draining and as everyone must know by now, stress is not just a bad thing, it is a killer. You must come up with ways to avoid it at all costs. Research has shown that stress can be a bit like a yawn, it can actually be contagious. In an earlier part we tackled "mirror neurons" that are signals produced in the brain that provide some degree of ability for us to absorb and comprehend other people's feelings and emotions.

In the same way that we might understand others, we can also be a huge "antenna," for receiving those around us who may send us all their bad stuff. Negative energy and stress can be incoming in this way. Science tells us that even as we observe another's anger, our stress hormones may rise up to twenty-six percent in our bodies. Stress conveyed to us through other people can show up in a variety of ways. When we spend time thinking about the problems that someone else may be experiencing or getting nervous or afraid because that is the emotion that another person close to us is feeling is a stress maker for all of us.

Also, sustained stress can give us all sorts of extended health issues which means we must find a way to protect ourselves from the "outside" sources of errant stress. The following are a few suggestions that may help to immunize you against secondhand stress:

1. Do not let stress spread into your body! As social individuals, we see, and we feel. Prevent unfavorable "other peoples" stress and negativity by focusing on your own current feelings. This will contain your emotions and show you that these new apparent "inputs" are not yours. Thereby keeping tabs on your good feelings.

2. Empathize without swallowing the entire pill yourself! We are in charge of us and they are in charge of them and this focus can be a great deal of help as a filter or boundary locator. Put up your fence and play on your side, let them play on their side. This is actually a good time to do a lesson within yourself and know your passions and your own empathy. It's okay to substantiate their situation and do listen to their words if they need to "get it out," but remember, don't jump right in and share the agony. This is just not necessary.

3. Monitor your own stress levels on a regular basis and don't let them rise up! Get the endorphins going and observe your breathing. Utilize your

mindfulness and meditate daily and if you can, multiple times a day. Any kind of exercise is also a great way to keep tabs on yourself. Your body will thank you when you pump up the body machine now and then.

4.   Monitor your sense of boundaries! In a way, checking in on your boundary patrol is a healthy thing to be doing. Simply be vigilant and always know when to step away from and individual or a situation.

5.   Boosting your sense of self, staying vigilant on boundary patrol, and monitoring your own feelings are all tools that can help to keep secondhand stress under control.

For the past few years, there has been a relatively new psychological theory in the works called "Emotional Intelligence." The idea is that just as people have an array of intellectual abilities, they also have a range of emotional abilities and skills. These emotional "tools," can be of immense assistance in the area of our thinking and what we do from day today.

The bottom line here is that utilizing this theory makes you a better person and can help you grow in ways that you want to grow and not wherever the wind may take you.

Ch6.Reducing Fear and Anxiety

Anxiety disorders are very common today, and it is estimated, according to data from several investigations, that 20% of the population will experience an anxiety crisis throughout their lives. One of the most known anxieties disorders are fears, among which we can highlight social fear. But what is social fear? What can we do to overcome it?

Fear is an emotion that has played a fundamental role in the survival of human beings. And also, this is fundamental in animals and in humans for survival. It mainly serves to guide us about the dangers that can threaten us at any given time, whether they are perceived in the external world or in the internal world. Activate in our body the escape or fight responses, as it is more convenient.

What Types of Fears Exist?

Simple fears generally occur towards a single object. They have a source, where they come from, usually in childhood, whereas children we get scared of certain things or situations. Being already adults and in similar scenarios, something acts as a trigger and makes us relive those terrifying feelings of the past, as if we were still small and helpless, developing a fear of something.

There are complex fears, which are related fears and intermingled with personality characteristics and character. They generally appear in the course of development in childhood or associated with various traumatic experiences in adolescence that intensify aspects already vulnerable in the first years of life. Mainly, they hinder the relationship with others, intimacy, commitment and aspects of self-concept, such as self-assessment. The social fear is an example of complex fears.

What Differentiates Fear from Shyness?

Shyness is a characteristic of introverted people, who are rather reserved, with a lot of inner life and who sometimes find it difficult to show themselves more socially, to appear, to have prominence and to develop socially with skills related to good conversation, to be entertaining or fun, Be the life of the party They are usually very thoughtful people with an intense emotional world that is little outwardly visible.

How Does Social Fear Affect the Lives of People Who Suffer from It?

It is very limiting. It can go so far as to make the person have to live in seclusion at home, avoiding contact with other people outside his family. Or also, it is observed when the person finds difficulties to attend usual social activities (study, work, shows) or exceptional (weddings, graduations).

The fear of being evaluated or being exposed is the predominant effect that these people experience, in addition to having many difficulties to show themselves publicly, to be the centre of attention of others or to stand out for some particular reason.

It is very great suffering that they suffer, reaching the extreme of not feeling worthy of being loved by others or having the feeling that there is a fault or a defect in them that they do not want others to see.

Social fear affects more in contexts with little appreciation of feelings, which are experienced as a sign of weakness, in environments of effective lack, where children are not offered safety experiences within the family so that later they become in children who succeed. Also in very overprotective and normative environments, where children do not develop self-affirmative feelings of their own value, where everything is resolved, and they do not have to work and put their own resources into play to get what they want.

A fear develops then to go out into the world, to connect with others as we are, with our defects and our virtues, to deal with our limitations to overcome those obstacles that arise. It may also happen that one of our caregivers in childhood has this same problem, and we learn somehow those fears or similar ones.

Anyway, even if we have grown up in an adverse environment, we can acquire from adults the security that we did not obtain in later rearing, develop new resources and strengthen ourselves to make our way into the external world. This sometimes occurs because there are new, more favorable contexts (partners, educational or sports contexts, a family of friends, gangs of university colleagues, work team) later in development or because people ask for specialized medical, psychiatric, help or psychological to overcome those difficulties.

In the case of complex fears, the treatments are longer since aspects related to the way of being and personality are worked, focusing on how to establish emotional ties and manage the emotional world.

One of the most commonly used techniques for the treatment of fears is systematic desensitization. Systematic desensitization consists of planning the very gradual and progressive exposure to those stimuli that produce the fear.

The person is developing the possibility of approaching what terrifies him with support at the beginning of the therapist, who sometimes acts as a counter phobic companion and through systematic repetitions, which increase the difficulty and time of exposure, it is justly desensitized, that is to say no longer feel fear and that the object of this fear becomes something non-frightening for the person.

Is It Possible to Overcome Fear Without Applying Exposure Techniques?

Of course. The exposure technique has been developed by the Cognitive Behavioral approach, and certain patients do very well and thus solve their problem.

But experts are very used to receiving people who have undergone this type of punctual treatment on a fear, based on exposure techniques, over time they develop another similar or the same intensifies, so it is necessary to apply here other types of targeted treatments at greater depth than allow the problem to work at its root, so that it does not reproduce again.

A person with social fear, or any other type of fear, can recover. You can return to experience much of its functionality, and you can develop roles and resources that allow you to go out into the world feeling safe and secure, safely and without fear, recovering a normal relationship with what generated so much fear.

Many times, patients are surprised to discover that something they have suffered for so long can remit resulting in new experiences and expanding the possibilities of experiences, which were previously not available.

In another perspective, social fear or social anxiety is a disorder in which people experience intense anxiety symptoms when they find themselves in social situations in which they irrationally fear feeling judged, humiliated or ridiculed.

A person with social fear cannot relate to or perform normal activities that involve being in a group, whether at work, at parties, or at sporting activities. Even acting in front of others also suffers, even if just to talk on the phone, ask for the bill or eat. It can be said that a person with social fear has an intense fear of relating

Zombies Representing the Social Fear

Although many people believe this is a kind of shyness, the truth is that social fear is not the same thing. A shy person experiences shame and, in some cases, fear, but in a very attenuated way; In fact, a certain degree of shyness is normal in most people. However, when suffering from social fear, the symptoms of anxiety and fear are disproportionately intense and disabling.

Physical symptoms experienced by a person with social fear can range from flushing, excessive sweating, dizziness and tremors, to nausea, gastrointestinal discomfort, tachycardia and even bouts of Anxiety. In addition, these symptoms are not limited to the time of social interaction, as one of the hallmarks of this disorder is exaggerated anticipation that causes people to live in states of anxiety weeks before each event they have to face.

The problem, as with other fears, is that in many cases, Anxiety leads people to avoid fearful situations, creating a vicious circle in which the main goal is to avoid relating.

Social fear impoverishes the life of the person who suffers it, making it difficult to find work, friends or partners and all kinds of experiences. In addition, whenever a situation that can trigger Anxiety is avoided, fear becomes stronger and more powerful.

Is It Possible to Get Out of the Vicious Circle of Social Fear?

Overcoming social fear is possible, but as with other anxiety problems, the road is long and requires commitment and effort. Recognizing and accepting the problem is the first step, but in most cases, it will be essential to seek professional help to overcome this disorder.

Some keys that can facilitate coping and managing social fear are as follows:

Be Aware of the Problem

Knowing what happens to us is the first step and then working with it. Now, it's important to be very clear that we are not the problem, but that we have a problem. Everyone has moments of weakness and overcoming. We all have the right to be nervous and make mistakes, and the important thing is to be on the road to overcome.

Working on self-esteem and self-acceptance is critical to overcoming social fear because it connects us with our essence and allows us to know ourselves. This will make it easier to accept what happens to us.

Face Fears Progressively

Moving to action is another key step. The important thing to overcome a fear is to face what is frightening but progressively. We can start practicing in environments that are not too hostile, such as in family gatherings, with a friend, or in small groups.

Another way to keep moving forward is to pursue our own challenges. If we are afraid of eating in public, we will try to take the snack until one day we are able to sit in the park to eat it. If we are afraid to participate in class, we will enroll in some activity where we know that there are few people to interact little by little. If what we fear is facing opinions, we can start by discussing a topic with a kind family member.

The key is to start little by little and move on to situations that generate the most Anxiety. Having a record of our achievements is very motivating.

How to Overcome Social Fear?

Learn to Manage Anxiety

Searching for our own ways to manage Anxiety will help us. For example, playing sports, meditating, or learning relaxation techniques... The less anxiety we experience, the less we will have to deal with at the most difficult times.

Seek Professional Help

If you feel that you cannot go it alone or that you need external support, do not hesitate to seek professional help.

Research has shown that cognitive-behavioral therapy, along with the development of social skills and techniques to control Anxiety, work to overcome social fear.

As we see, social fear is a limiting problem that impoverishes our relationships, but one that we can progressively overcome if we strive. Above all, we need to try.

Ch7.Channeling Your Unique Energy into Your Life

We all have natural gifts and talents. Some individuals are artistic, some are sporty or adventurous, and some are empaths. No gift should ever be hidden; following your passions is a way of finding purpose in life, which is something we all need to thrive. Consider some abilities that your gift has given you that you maybe weren't even aware of.

Empathetic Listening

Empathetic listening is truly understanding and being able to perceive what someone is saying to you. There is absolutely no judgment involved, but only raw compassion and understanding. Empathetic listening is not always easy as it means putting all your own personal needs and opinions aside to focus on who really needs your support. It's not necessarily about giving advice but about lending an ear to someone in need. Empaths are able to do this far easier than others, and, in fact, many empaths become psychologists and counselors because of it.

How comforting is the thought of having a space to release your emotions in a safe environment? This is exactly what someone with the gift of empathetic listening provides. It requires a certain level of thoughtfulness between the two individuals involved and can definitely create a bond. Through using their gift, empaths improve their ability to understand and console, which strengthens them in many aspects of their lives.

Attentiveness is given to what is being said, and this will make the individual feel important and cared for. It releases tension and can improve the mood, which is one of the things an empath lives for. The other person won't have to worry about being interrupted while releasing your emotions as an empathetic listener will constantly reassure them during the process. When someone's needs are put first and acknowledged, it increases their confidence and will forge a positive light on speaking up about how they feel in the future. It can never be a bad thing to be able to openly and honestly voice your thoughts.

Through empathetic listening, an empath can truly help someone in need. This is definitely a gift to be proud of. Use it often and you will never be without loved ones.

Empathetic Leading

Empathetic leading is sometimes viewed as a weak trait, but this is most definitely not the case. To be a good leader, sometimes it is required that you be able to put yourself in the other person's shoes for a moment. Empathetic leaders are also generally empathetic listeners as it is beneficial to them to be able to intently listen and understand the needs of those around them. Empaths that are in charge of others mostly don't have the "do as I say" attitude and are emotional thinkers which might seem like a poor skill to some, but in fact, is a unique kind of strength. If there is one thing that people being led by someone else want to feel, it is equality. Empathetic leaders make those around them feel like equals by considering them in every aspect of decision-making.

Empathetic leaders can use their gift to their advantage in more ways than one. They are able to use out the bad apples and pick up on some things that may be sketchy. They might even use the knowledge of someone else's feelings and emotions in a way that is beneficial to them if they deem it necessary.

The gift of being an empathetic leader is that those under you are likely to truly respect you and your opinions. It creates loyalty and clear communication, which helps to improve overall work ethic. The ability to put yourself in someone else's shoes is a fantastic one.

Empathetic Relationships

No relationship is ever perfect. For one to succeed, it requires effort from each partner, many sacrifices, and a lot of forgiveness. Above all else, you need to be able to compromise. If your partner is an empath, you may be much luckier than you think. They can be very difficult people to understand and deal with at times, but they have the traits that make up some of the best life partners.

Empaths are unbelievably loyal to their loved ones. They only wish to see the best in their partners, and they will give their partners their whole heart and soul. You see, when empaths dedicate themselves to something, they go all in. This includes relationships. You will be the main focus point in their lives, and they will do anything to make sure you know that you are loved and cared for. They are the type of people that will move mountains even if all they get back in return is a smile. Once they have devoted themselves to you, they will love unconditionally. This love is one of the purest forms you will ever find.

Since an empath's emotions and feelings are so intense, they are able to love just as deeply. They feel very passionately and will never deliberately hurt you as it would cause them great upset. They can often use their gift to read the situation and get a gauge on how you are feeling. When angry, they are very careful when selecting their words as they will not say anything to worsen a situation because their gift allows them to understand the situation on a deeper level. Openness and honesty are high up on the list of what empaths find important, and when they trust you, they will not do anything to hide their thoughts and fears from you. They are able to bring out the best in you through their joy and happiness and the optimism is only beneficial in a partner's life.

When an empath feels the pain of their partner, their natural healing instincts will come out, and they will do anything to subdue the pain and protect you. Some may not realize it, but with an empath by your side, you will possess the ability to make the world a better place. They are able to understand you on a different level due to their amazing ability to feel what you are feeling.

Change Your Mindset

I believe that success and happiness are all about our mindsets. It affects everything in our lives, even how we react and handle the world around us. To achieve your goals, you need your mindset to level up with your aspirations.

The Path to Self-Improvement

Your self-talk has a direct connection with whether or not you have a positive or negative mindset. Consider changing your negative self-talk into a full-on empowerment speech. Who better to encourage you than yourself? It'll have the biggest impact. One of the ways you can do this is by using the positive affirmations I mentioned earlier.

Your mindset is also a reflection of how you see yourself. If you constantly believe, for example, that you're a slob or a bad worker, you will eventually train your brain into believing and following these thoughts. Through reading, you might be surprised at how quickly you pick up on the author's way of thinking. Look into some literature that will lead you in the right direction and try to avoid dark and heavy reading until you're in a better headspace. Reading is an excellent activity for an empath to take up due to their ability to see how others feel and think. You may find that books help you feel more positive, depending on their genres and titles. Go for self-motivating and happy books and take note of how much your mindset changes by journaling.

Using your environment to exercise your way of thinking is maybe one of the best options for an empath. We tend to forget that there is a lot more out there than little old us when trapped in a certain mindset. You might think you're stuck in the worst situation possible until you see someone else in an even worse predicament than yourself. Nature can be your getaway and "mind cleanser" when you really need it. There is nothing like beautiful scenery to readjust your way of thinking and make you appreciate the beauty of this world and life. As a bonus, sunshine is fantastic for a natural mood-booster. Once your head is clear again, you can carry on with your self-improvement journey. Sometimes all we need is a bit of a break from our own minds in order to get back on track. There's no better break than a walk-in nature. You could even take that book along.

Surround yourself with people that have your desired mindset and try to celebrate your daily small achievements in life; it will lead you to accomplishing many more.

You Are Good Enough

Trust me, everyone on the planet has had a moment where they felt like they weren't good enough. Worse than that, I believe all of us have let the words and thoughts of others dictate how we feel about ourselves. No one can make you feel that way if you do not let them. Ultimately, you are in charge of your feelings and thoughts. Do not let anyone take that away from you.

A perfect example of what can make us feel like we're not good enough is the opinions of others and that little voice in our own head.

Shut down your inner critic. He's not doing you any good. You can talk back. The moment that little voice starts nagging at you about something that makes you feel inferior, shut it down. By shifting your focus onto something else or just simply saying "no," you are training yourself to recognize your self-worth. Make a list of what boosts your confidence on those days that you just aren't able to get rid of that voice. Perhaps you should consider saving or writing down messages that someone said that put a smile on your face. If they're truly worth it, stick them up somewhere you'll see them often, like the bathroom mirror.

It is so easy to compare ourselves to others on a daily basis as we always want to be the best that we can possibly be. The hard truth is that there is always going to be someone better than you. There will always be someone smarter, faster, or more attractive. You need to make peace with it, or it will eat you up inside. You don't need to be better than everyone else. You only need to be you. Trust me, being you is a pretty great thing. Being the best, you are what is important, not being better than someone else.

Social media is one of the things that is a major cause of people not feeling good enough about themselves.

Many of us have at least one social media account and it is incredibly difficult to avoid, particularly since they are designed to be addictive

Ch8.

Being Yourself and

Allow Your Creative Side to Flourish

Be Your Own First Priority

If you are completely drained, you will not be able to deal with the struggles of daily life or handle normal interactions with people. Even a person who's not an empath will struggle to control their emotions when they are exhausted and depleted. This is much worse for empaths, as they are dealing with their own emotions, as well as the emotions of the people and energy around them. Putting yourself first is not a selfish act. This is difficult for empaths to accept, but when they put this into practice, they will realize its importance.

Build Fences, Not Walls

Empaths tend to isolate themselves to prevent being overwhelmed by the emotions and energies of others. Don't do this! By all means, take time alone to decompress when you need to, but there is no reason that you can't have a healthy, active social life and be successful at work.

You can and should support the people in your life. However, it is important that you do not give them all your energy. You will be a better friend and a family member and lead a more meaningful life if you are not depleted. To accomplish this, you need to develop boundaries.

If you have a coworker who is draining for you to be around, you can still work with them. But you do not need to socialize outside of the workplace. If they invite you to lunch, politely decline. Use the excuse that you have to work for lunch. Next time tell them that you brought lunch, or you are on a special diet. They will eventually get the hint. Keep your interactions with co-workers you find draining limited to what is necessary for your job. On days that you know you'll need to spend a lot of time with them for professional reasons, take some extra time for yourself in the morning to practice self-care. Make sure you take the time that evening to decompress.

If you feel your life would be better without a certain person in your life, you should cut them out of your life. For example, you may have a friend from your childhood that always needs something from you and always has problems they want you to solve but is who never there for you in return. Someone like this can be extremely draining for anyone to maintain a friendship with but is even more difficult for an empath. Empaths have a harder time saying no. It is harder to cut a conversation short. But if someone is bringing toxicity into your life, don't feel that you have to keep them in it just because you have a shared history. If this feels too selfish, try to reframe how you think about it: you will have a lot of time and energy to help other people if this toxic person is no longer in your life. Your friend will be better off if they have a friend without empathic abilities who is not so drained being around them. They can find another toxic person, and they can be toxic together.

For people, such as family members that you cannot cut out of your life, you should set clearly defined boundaries. For example, you may have a sister who you love dearly, but who is so needy that you always feel very drained after interacting with her. In this example, you could set boundaries such as limiting the time you spend with the person or on the phone. Your boundaries may be that you end your daily phone call after ten minutes and schedule a two-hour brunch every other week. Your boundaries should be based on your relationship with the person and how much interacting with them drains you.

At a certain time, each evening, turn off your phone or at least silence the ringer. Let your friends and family know that after this time of night, you are unavailable, except in emergencies. Don't be afraid to tell them that you consider an emergency a health crisis or similar. Your younger sister's fifteenth breakup with the same man she keeps going back to is not an emergency under this paradigm. You can talk to her about this the next day during your ten-minute phone call. You can support the people in your life and be there for them without being at the beck and call.

Many empaths find that touch intensifies the emotions they are experiencing through others and increases energy absorption. When you are in a crowd, you can try to navigate the edges, so you aren't bumping into as many people. You can give shorter hugs when you greet friends. You don't want to close yourself off completely to touch, but some people are just not as physically affectionate as others. Being one of them is fine. If you are meeting a lot of new people and want to avoid shaking hands, mention you feel like you have a cold coming on. People will appreciate the warning and keep their hands to themselves. Once you learn to shield yourself, you will not have to worry about making these excuses.

If you are in a social situation and are feeling intense vibes from someone that are making you uncomfortable or upset, you can move away. Do this kindly and unobtrusively. No one will think your behavior is odd or antisocial if you politely excuse yourself to refill a beverage, get some food, or use the restroom. If you are in a waiting room, you can always move seats. Grab your things, make a phone call outside, or ask the receptionist a question. When you return, simply sit elsewhere. Most people self-absorbed enough to not even notice.

Practice Separation

Empaths feel the emotions of others as strongly as they do their own. But it is important to remember that these emotions you are feeling through others aren't yours. They don't reflect what you are experiencing in your life. If your best friend is going through a divorce, the anger and sadness you are feeling through them is not your anger and sadness. Be there for your friend. Do your best to help and support them, but do not let their situation subsume you.

To practice separation, you first need to acknowledge the emotions you are feeling. Then, you mentally compartmentalize them as belonging to your friend and release them. Allow yourself to decompress and clear your mind after interacting with this friend.

Understand Your Own Emotions

Once you have separated the emotions you are experiencing through other people, it's time to concentrate on your own emotions. We'll continue with the example of an empath who has a friend going through a divorce. When you have released the anger and sadness you are feeling through them, think about your relationship. Do you have a significant other? How do you feel about the relationship? Does your partner make you happy and enhance your life? If you are single, are you content with this or do you want a relationship? What do you need and want in a partner? What do you expect to get out of being in a relationship?

Discover how you are feeling in your own life. Acknowledge and understand your emotions.

Determine the source of these emotions. If you are sad, figure out why. Sometimes, the source will be obvious; other times, you will have to delve deeper. When you are more aware of your life and emotions, it will make it easier for you to separate your emotions from the emotions you feel through other people. Journaling can be a great way to examine your emotions, as well as practicing separation.

Are you happy? What can make you happier? Are you depressed? Why? What can you do to make it better? You give so much support to the people in your life; don't be afraid to ask them for support if you need it! You may decide you would benefit from therapy to further explore your emotions.

Release Responsibility

Empaths often feel they carry the weight of the world. They burden themselves with the suffering and problems of others. Empaths feel extreme guilt for not being able to fix other people's problems. You are not responsible for other people's problems. It's not your fault your best friend is struggling through a divorce. You cannot fix it. You would be overstepping your bounds to attempt to do so. You must let those around you live their own life and make their own decisions. This includes letting them make their own mistakes. You can actually do people a disservice by not allowing them to fend for themselves. They need to learn to rely on themselves and their own strength, not just yours. Concentrate on your own life and your own path.

If it is hard for you to change your mindset from fixing people to supporting them, consider that by controlling your empath abilities, you are allowing the people in your life to have privacy. You wouldn't want someone to read your every emotion. You can consider shielding a form of respect.

If you receive information through intuition that you feel it's imperative to share, be respectful of how the other person receives your information. You may get a bad feeling around your friend's significant other. If you choose to share this with your friend, be prepared that they won't want to hear it and they may be angry with you for telling them. You can tell them why you feel this way, but don't tell them what to do.

Celebrate!

There is a lot of pain and sadness in the world. This can weigh particularly heavily on empaths, who experience so much emotional pain that is not their own. Don't wait for holidays to celebrate the good things, whether large or small. Take the time to celebrate and bring joy into your life and the lives of those around you. If you got a promotion at work, treat yourself to a nice dinner. If you accomplished a workout goal, buy yourself a new training outfit. Is your 40th birthday coming up? Throw yourself a birthday bash! No "over the hill" paraphernalia allowed—good vibes only! Host a dinner party just because you have a new recipe you want to try.

Ch9.Using Your Gift to Your Advantage

To develop the gifts and talents of empaths, experts recommend a two-step approach: read properly the emotions of others and show how much you understand them. Take note that each step is dependent on one another. By doing these steps as a cyclic process, you would be able to significantly improve your empathic abilities.

Reading the Emotions of Other People

The first aspect of empathy that you can develop is your ability to read and understand the emotions of those around you. There are numerous ways on how you could go about this, but the main goal for every one of them is to gain an awareness of how another person might be feeling. Though reading the emotions of others is not an exact science—given the complexities of human nature—you would still be able to get valuable information that would help you learn how to act and think like a highly empathic individual.

To truly understand other people, you need to have the ability to recognize where they are coming from and figure out how they think and feel. Showing others that you are capable of this is usually a disarming experience for them. When you manage to disarm them, they would be more likely to take off their masks and share with you their real thoughts and feelings. Only then would you be able to offer the help that they actually need from others.

In a way, highly empathic individuals are selfless beings. They step out of their comfort zones to totally immerse themselves in the lives of other people. They are willing to open up themselves in order to figure out how to make things better for those around them.

So, how would you be able to walk in the shoes of another person? One of the most recommended methods by experts is a three-prong approach. The main objective, however, is to read between the lines. Listen to what others have to say but focus on how they are saying it. By doing this, you would be able to get a more accurate image of the person before you.

- Analyzing the Words of Other People

Highly empathic individuals are effective listeners. They are able to pay attention to what the other person is saying, and from there, pick out the points that really matter. They are not just listening to what others have to say. They are also processing as well as the information that they are receiving at the same moment.

There are times when words do not align with what the other person truly means. As such, empath needs to figure out what the other person is hinting at. Taking your listening skills to the next level needs time and practice. To make this process easier for you, do this exercise with someone you already know, and who is willing to tell you if your observations are accurate or not.

- First, let your partner speak about whatever topic that he or she wants to talk about at that given moment. Do not converse with your partner. Instead, just focus and listen to what they have to say.

For example, your partner, Anna, chooses to talk about her personal issues with her husband, Ben. Apparently, Anna wants to have kids, but Ben does not. Anna says that at first, it bothered her, but now she thinks it does not matter anymore.

• As you listen to her, take note of any emotion seeping through the tone of her voice. Check if there is any contradiction between her tone and the words, she is saying.

Following the same scenario given above, when Anna said that the issue is not bothering her anymore, you picked up the disappointment in the tone of her voice. Your ears heard her words correctly, but your intuition as an empath tells you that there is something else going on.

• Reflect on the meaning of the words of your partner and analyze them against the tone of her voice. Given the melody and rhythm of her voice, you believe that Anna still wants to have to kids and that she feels frustrated over her husband's refusal to have them in the future.

You can empathize with her by acknowledging her true feelings. Do not question the accuracy of her words. Instead, focus on what she truly feels to show that you understand the underlying meaning of her words.

When you have managed to say something back that correctly reflects the true meaning of your partner's words, the relationship between the two of you becomes closer. A deeper bond would begin to form since your partner would believe that you get where she is coming from. Continue practicing your skills as an intuitive listener so that you would be able to form more accurate conclusions about what people truly mean with their words.

• Understanding the Facial Expressions of Other People

Speaking to another person involves not only your ears but also your eyes. You have to observe the facial cues in order to get a fuller understanding of what others are saying. Even when someone is silent, their faces usually give away what they are really thinking or feeling at a given moment.

To help you practice this skill, here is a list of facial features that you need to observe, and the corresponding meanings of the common expressions that you might notice as you do so.

- Eyes

The eyes are a good source of information for empaths since most of its movements are automatic responses rather than controlled or deliberate. By observing them, you would be able to get a better idea of where the other person is coming from.

If a person's gaze is steady and does not back away when you stare back at him or her, then the person is likely not hiding anything away from you. If you two are conversing, then he or she believes in what you are saying.

On the other hand, a person who averts his or her gaze from you is most likely feeling worried about something. That person may also be hiding something, and he or she feels anxious that you would be able to uncover it. If someone's gaze shifts away whenever you make eye contact with him or her, it could either be an act of anxiety or avoidance.

- Eyebrows

The position of the eyebrows is indicative of a person's feelings. According to experts, human eyebrows move not only when the person is feeling happy or sad, but also whenever someone feels an extreme emotion in reaction to stimuli or information.

For instance, when the eyebrows are raised, the person could either be feeling surprised or curious. However, depending on the context of the situation, this position could also be taken as a sign of relief.

If the eyebrows are lowered, it could mean either that the person is experiencing displeasure, or that the person is trying to hide away something from others. The position is seen as an unintentional act of hiding one's gaze, similar to when the eyes dart away from the gaze of other people.

- Forehead

Check if the forehead of the person you are observing is wrinkled or smooth. If someone is deep in thought or confused, the forehead tends to become wrinkled. Smooth foreheads indicate that the person is feeling at ease or unbothered.

Signs of sweating on the forehead are also something that you should look out for. If the weather is not particularly warm, sweating on the forehead or any other part of the face could mean that the person is feeling anxious.

- Mouth

Observe if the person is exhibiting signs of a smile or frown. This is pretty telling of a person's true emotions, not just, because smiles and frowns are usually associated with happiness and sadness, respectively. If the emotion expressed in the eyes and mouth do not match, then the person is likely trying to hide his or her true feelings about someone or a certain situation.

To increase your level of empathy, try to practice reading the facial expressions of someone who can tell how accurate you are. However, please note that any variances between the expression and the words of a person do not mean that the person is deliberately doing it. Sometimes, a person is unaware of their facial expressions or what they are truly feeling.

Explaining how you have come about your conclusions is a more effective approach. Rather stating it like a fact, it would also be helpful if you would adopt a questioning tone when you try to assess someone's facial expressions. Here are some following guide questions that you could use for this:

- Are you feeling anxious right now?

- Do you feel happy about that?

- Is that bothering you?

- Do my words upset you?

- Decoding the Body Language of Other People

Beyond one's facial expression, a person's body language is also a veritable source of information for empaths. People with high levels of empathy are able to turn this information into a deeper understanding of the people around them.

Here is a list of tips on how you can effectively decode the meanings of one's bodily gestures:

- If a person is feeling comfortable or dominant, he or she would usually adopt an open posture—head is held up; the body is facing forward; arms extended outwards, or arms kept at the person's sides).

- A person who feels inferior exhibits a closed body posture, wherein he or she has her arms folded while facing away.

- A person leaning forwards shows that he or she is interested. If coupled with a tense body, it could mean that the person is feeling angry instead.

- If the shoulders are drooping, the person is likely feeling sad or tired.

- A body that is facing away can be indicative of a person's anxiety, embarrassment, or shyness.

- One can adopt a welcoming posture by standing or sitting with arms opened up towards other people.

- On the other hand, arms crossed in front of the body signals that the person is feeling defensive over something or towards someone.

Showing Others That You Understand Their Feelings

The other empathic ability that you can develop is your ability to show others that you understand their feelings. The timing and the manner of expressing this separates a highly empathic person from other people with average or low empathy.

Again, it is best to practice this with a person that you are close with. Learn how to pace yourself as well. Starting too intensely would make the other person feel uncomfortable. You can try to practice first with minor inconveniences of day-to-day to life.

Ch10.Controlling Your Awareness of Feelings and Emotions

The first step when it comes to the emotions you are feeling, no matter where they came from, is acknowledging how you feel. Think of it this way, before you can start to heal from any situation in your life, you need to acknowledge it. You need to stand up and say, "This is how I am feeling" before you can start to understand why you are feeling this way. For example, you are hanging out with friends when you see a commercial about dogs in shelters. A local shelter is asking people from the community to adopt these dogs because their shelter is becoming too full. While some of the dogs look happily at the camera, one dog is curled up in a corner shaking. As you see this dog you say, "Oh, that poor puppy! He looks so scared and sad. It just makes me want to run up and hug him. No one should ever have to feel that way." In response, one of your friends laughs and says, "It's just part of the commercial. It's all so they grab the attention of people like you." You look at your friend and then start to feel self-conscious about what you said out loud. No one else seems to be reacting in the same way. You start to feel a little embarrassed as you look down at your phone thinking to yourself, "You need to be more careful of what you say out loud. Not everyone thinks like you do."

Throughout the rest of the evening, you are not as sociable with your friends. When they are laughing and having fun, you tend to give them a smile. You don't laugh as much because you don't feel like it. You start to get lost in your thoughts as you wonder what is causing you to withdraw from your friends. Why do you still feel bothered by what your friend said to you in response to your reaction to the commercial? You feel that other people would be move on from the situation and continue to have a good time, but you feel more out of place. How could you feel out of place amongst your friends?

The truth is you don't necessarily feel out of place with your friends. You know that they never mean to harm you emotionally or psychologically. What you are struggling with is acknowledging how your friend made you feel. You haven't acknowledged the embarrassment you felt. You haven't looked at the words they said that caused you to feel ashamed about the way you reacted to the commercial. When you don't acknowledge the way you feel, especially as an empath and highly sensitive person, you will hang on to the situation for a period of time.

Four Steps of Acknowledging Your Emotions

1.   Note how you are truly feeling. People quickly try to push feelings aside. This is more common if you were not allowed to talk about your feelings or you didn't have parents teaching you how to open up as a child. This type of behavior will follow you into adulthood. It is also easy to tell yourself, "I feel kind of sad" and then not look deeper into the feeling.

2.   Reflect on your feelings. You want to think about why you feel this way. Ask yourself when it started to find the possible source of your emotions.

Take time to write down how you feel and why as this can help you process your emotions.

3. Stay open to your emotions. There is nothing wrong with vulnerability as it will help you be honest and open about how you are feeling. This isn't information that you need to share with anyone else, unless you want to. The important part is you stay open with yourself and begin to work through your emotions.

4. Go with the flow. You need to let your emotion run its course. Sometimes it will be painful, and this is something that is tough to get through. However, you cannot move on without fully acknowledging your emotion. It can take time to go through your emotion and you will find yourself wishing that you could forget about it and feel better. You won't feel better until you fully acknowledge the way you are feeling.

Understanding Your Emotions

Once you acknowledge your emotions, you need to start to understand your emotions. You will start this process when you begin to reflect on your feelings. To begin understanding your emotions, you need to know the five core emotions:

1.   Hurt

2.   Anger

3.   Fear

4.   Sadness

5.   Joy

Any other emotions, such as guilt or jealousy, are known as secondary emotions. Secondary emotions are combinations of the core emotions. For example, you can feel hurt and anger when you are feeling jealous or fear and sadness when you are feeling guilty.

One of the first factors to know about understanding your emotions is that they don't always need to be positive. Like most people, you have no problem understanding your positive emotions. Positive emotions make you feel content and calm. They give you an uplifting feeling which helps you get through your day. When you feel negatively, you start to feel down. This has psychological effects, especially if you don't understand your negative emotions. For example, you meet your friend at the restaurant and see your ex-partner with someone else. While you have your own significant other, you still feel jealous seeing them. You see your ex is happy with their partner and you begin to wonder why you couldn't do the same for them. You are also confused with your emotions because it was your decision to end the relationship. If it was your choice, why do you feel jealous seeing your ex with someone else?

As a child, you let your emotions run wild. When you were unhappy, you let people know and you didn't see a problem with this. As you grew up, you started to scale your emotions back because you learned it isn't okay to be too emotional. This happens for different reasons. It might be because your parents told you to not act emotional or because society told you acting this way is bad. Now, to understand your emotions, you need to bring them back into the front. The only way you can understand where they come from and why you feel a certain way is by focusing on your emotions and the situation. To understand your emotions, you will ask yourself a variety of questions. For example, what happened before you started to feel this way? Is there something with your past that caused this emotion to come to the surface? For example, you are working in your office and you hear two of your co-workers talking about another co-worker negatively. You try to ignore the conversation but struggle to do so because it makes you angry. You don't understand how someone could be mean, especially when they work with someone five days out of the week. You don't feel the judgements from your co-workers is justified. You try to ignore your anger because it doesn't make sense to you. Your co-workers weren't talking to you, they weren't talking about you, and you don't know the co-worker they talked about well. Unfortunately, you are unable to ignore the anger as it continues to bubble up within you. On the way home from work, you start to think about the situation. You ask yourself, "Why did I get so angry?" and immediately think of the bullying you dealt with as a child in school. Therefore, you think this is one of the biggest reasons you feel so angry is because of the bullying.

Three Ways to Better Understand Your Emotions

There are many ways that you can start to understand your emotions better. For instance, you can use your own techniques that you develop over time. To help you start to understand your emotions better, here are three steps to follow (David, 2016).

1.   Note the intensity of your emotion. You want to understand how strong your emotion is. For example, if you are feeling angry, do you have certain levels of anger? Do you feel like you could emotionally explode and yell at someone or are you more frustrated about the situation, like something is working right for you? To help you understand your intensity, rate them on a scale of one to ten.

2.   Expand your emotional vocabulary. Like everyone, you know the words angry, frustrated, sad, happy, and fear. But there are many other words that can express the way you feel. For example, you can

also describe angry as annoyed, disgusted, irritated, boiling, grumpy, and spiteful. You could describe happy as comfortable, thankful, content, elated, excited, and relieved. When you expand your emotional vocabulary, you can use different words when you make your emotional intensity scale.

3.   Write about your emotions. Writing is an important part of not only acknowledging your emotions but also understanding them. There is a positive connection between writing and your emotions. No matter how you feel, writing about your emotions can help you overcome any negative emotions and understand them better. You don't always need to ask yourself questions. You can free write, which is when you write whatever comes to your mind.

Controlling Your Emotions

Once you acknowledge and understand your emotions, you can start to control them. There are many strategies that will help you stay in control of your emotions throughout any situation.

•   Don't react immediately. Allow yourself to think about the situation before you react. For example, take a few deep and slow breaths to clear your mind. This will allow you to think rationally instead of jumping to conclusions.

•   Understand your triggers. Generally, people feel happy and calm. However, this can quickly change at any moment because everyone has emotional triggers. You will start to find out what your triggers are when you are acknowledging and understanding your emotions. By knowing your triggers, you can further control your emotions as you will start to understand where they come from and prepare yourself when the situation arises.

•   Change your thoughts. The biggest problem with negative emotions is they bring negative thoughts. This can create a cycle that you will struggle to get out of, so it is important that you replace your negative thoughts with positive thoughts. This doesn't mean that you want to ignore your negative emotions and thoughts. Always go through the points of acknowledging and understanding them as this will help you with control.

No matter what strategy you use, the point is to control your emotions, so they don't control you.

Absorbing Emotions

One of the biggest reasons empaths struggle with emotions is because they absorb emotions from other people. This means that the emotions people have when they are near you, you take on as your own. This is an important part of being an empath and a factor that you don't want to ignore because it helps you focus on healing other people. absorbing

Ch11. The Pros and Cons of Being an Empath

Depending how long you've known that you are an empath, you may be quite familiar with the pros and cons of being one. We've already covered that one of the downfalls can be the way it is a heavy burden to bear due to the outside energies and emotions you are surrounded by. However, most things in life come with both negatives and positives. The experience of feeling those emotions around you can be wonderful and helpful in many different ways.

The pros and cons can't really be separated as they are often intertwined with one another.

Empaths are listeners. They can be all sorts of joy, being outgoing and enthusiastic and generally bubbly. Let's not forget the heyoka empath literally known for being humorous when you least expect it. Their journey can be one of emotional bliss, but it can also be one of emotional turmoil since empaths can be weighed down with mood swings galore. This is because their moods are not always their own. If empaths don't fully understand and differentiate their own thoughts and feelings from those of others, they can have fluctuating mood swings that literally change with the speed of flicking a switch on and off.

As with the good, being an empath can come with feelings of depression, anxiety, panic, fear, and sorrow. Without having any control over these feelings, you can be experiencing the suffering of others. It's a very difficult thing to have to handle and shouldn't be done so alone.

This is where compassion comes in. An empath should have at least one person they can turn to in the throes of these mood swings because being left alone can be detrimental to mental and physical health. Find someone, be it a friend or a partner or a family member, who you can turn to when things get too overwhelming for you. Whoever you find, make sure to tell them that all you really need from them is empathic love—the ability to show compassion without judging you. This may help you in recovery from these overwhelming moments.

Most empaths, unless they have gone on their own journeys of self-discovery and self-acceptance, don't actually know or understand what's going on within. They don't know that they're feeling another person's emotions like they are their own emotions. This can quite obviously lead to a myriad of feelings such as confusion, particularly if things were grand in one moment and terrible in the next. Understanding their empathic connection is a part of the journey.

It's easier for an empath to withhold their feelings and emotions than it is for others. They want to do their best not to be barraged by the feelings and emotions of others. In doing so, they often become reclusive and learn to block out these feelings. The downside of this is that they can end up bottling up their own emotions or building walls so high that they don't ever let anyone else in. This can definitely be bad for an empath—or anyone for that matter—because the longer you allow these feelings and emotions to build up inside yourself, the more power they build up. Eventually, they can explode and leave behind a lot of damage to both the empath and those around the empath. This can create an unstable environment, a mental/emotional breakdown, and/or an actual disease.

Expressing yourself honestly is a choice, but it is a great form of healing.

Cons of Being an Empath

Some of these can count as pros depending on how you look at them. You'll notice how short this list is compared to the list of pros. This is because being an empath is truly a positive blessing if you understand your gift properly.

• You are easily overwhelmed. Wherever there are lots of people, you can be overwhelmed with the feelings and emotions emanating off of those that surround you. Sometimes you can be in a room with one person and still feel this way. This is why it is so important not to bottle things up.

• Addictive personalities. Empaths are prone to looking for ways to escape or block out the emotions of others. This means that they sometimes turn toward addictive substances such as sex, drugs, and alcohol. Learning to protect yourself and your energy means that you won't be struck with the need to escape these things. Instead, you will know how to cope with them properly.

• Media can be devastating. Some empaths turn away from media altogether. They can feel the emotions of others so strongly that even reading a newspaper is too much for them. It is a harsh world out there.

• Empaths can pick up both mental and physical ailments that others may suffer from. This can happen even if you don't come into contact with the other person, depending on how strong your gift is. Needless to say, no one wants to suffer this way.

• Intuition can be hurtful when you know that someone you care about is lying to you or keeping secrets from you. The ability to know and feel these things can be difficult, particularly if you can't prove such things. Try to surround yourself with people who are like minded preventing feeling this way on a regular basis.

•   We don't really have a home. Empaths are natural wanderers. After a certain amount of time, we can often feel foreign in places we once cherished. Our intuition implores with us to explore the great big world. Due to this, we're rarely ever satisfied with one place, but it does mean we make brilliant travelers.

Pros of Being an Empath

Well, we covered the cons, which I admit were pretty bad. Now we get to look at the reasons why being an empath truly is a gift. Bear with me here, because it's a pretty long list of reasons.

•   Empaths are natural healers in many different forms: emotional, physical, environmental, animal, you name it. They can use their touch, their voice, and their creativity to do so. Most empaths end up on a path of healing because they simply have that pull toward their profession.

• As tough as crowds may be for an empath, the small circle they often end up building for themselves is a strong one. Once an empath makes a connection with someone, they are incredibly loyal and loving. We hold onto our loved ones tightly because we don't want to let the good ones go.

• Okay, we already know this one, but empaths love an insane amount. Their hearts are just bigger than most. Being so overloaded with all these feelings makes faking them difficult.

• That gut instinct is extremely strong and if you listen to it, I'm pretty sure you could conquer the world if you wanted to. Listen to that sixth sense of yours because it could save you from potential dangers if it hasn't already.

• Along with having an extremely strong sense of intuition, we also have amazing senses. It isn't only emotions and feelings that are heightened. If you find yourself enjoying a myriad of sensations with a lot more intensity than those around you, you can chalk that up to being an empath. We have heightened senses that allow us to better enjoy our food, beverages, flowers, essential oils, touch, and so forth. Admittedly, these can sometimes overwhelm us, but they could also help save lives. How, you might ask? Well, if you work on increasing a certain sense, such as smell, you could be able to track down death or disease in animals, people, and/or nature.

• I know we said that the weight of other people's emotions is a burden and we're really prone to lows, but we've also got the other end of the spectrum. We have great highs, too. Most empaths actually have a deep enthusiasm for life, and when we are enjoying it, we experience joy intensely.

• Empaths have an abundance of creativity! We think and see things differently. Our art is not the only creative aspect of our life, but so are our experiences, situations, and prospects. Now, you've probably had the misfortune of being told that the way you think about and/or do things is wrong, but it's a capacity all your own. Don't let anyone take that unusual creativity away from you, and let it shine brightly instead.

• This Is yet another con that also turns out to be a pro, but we can't be lied to. We are good at reading people's thoughts, feelings, and emotions. This means that we can tell when people are lying, we can tell when people aren't okay, and we can tell when people are bad news.

• Empaths can read emotional and nonverbal cues really well. It's a talent in numerous places. Due to our good senses, we can even sense the needs of those who do not speak, such as animals and plants, but also the body and babies.

• An empath generally has a craving to make the world a better place. This isn't a desire that you should ever feel ashamed of. We are capable of bringing plenty of positive changes to this world, and when we can, we should. There are already too many people turning blind eyes. Let's work on correcting the wrongs happening around us—together.

- It's especially important for us to change the world considering our pull to it. We are children of nature. It's one of the best ways to de-stress, and it can provide peace and comfort.

- To some, this might seem more like a con, but find that it's pretty cool to be able to recharge on our own. We require a certain level of alone time to recuperate. It is because of this that we are self-aware and think it's great to be self-aware.

Conclusion

While this book is dedicated to helping those, who suffer from debilitating negative emotions, it is also highly beneficial for those who just want to gain a better awareness of themselves. By practicing self-reflection exercises, increasing your self-awareness, and constantly turning your negative experiences into more positive ones, you allow yourself to not only master your emotions, but become a master over your entire life.

Once you begin to live a life that allows you to have so much control of your actions and reactions, you will question what was so challenging about it before. In spite of the fact that it can require some investment to build up the aptitudes and actualize the procedures, this time is all around spent and you get back beyond what you would ever conceivable put in. An existence of enthusiastic opportunity is conceivable, and you get the opportunity to settle on the decision to live it once you settle on the decision to control what is keeping you down.

When you show compassion and kindness to others, you increase your own happiness. Acts of kindness can take the form of many things — whether it is being more generous with your money, time, affection, or other resources, giving creates more positive emotions, which results in more pleasant feelings. Consider ways you can give more in each area, such as:

- Volunteering

- Scheduling one-on-one, uninterrupted time with your kids

- Treating someone to lunch

- Educating others

- Being more involved in your community

It can be easy to overlook the many ways you can express more kindness. Even something as simple as holding the door open for someone, buying coffee for the person behind you in line, or just smiling at others not only have a significant impact on the other person's life, but will also help you feel better about yours. In most cases, doing random acts of kindness on a daily basis creates a ripple effect, where the person you were kind to, be then kind to the next person, and so on. Just this thought alone can help cultivate more positive feelings.

Learn to really listen

Consider how much better you feel when you are having a conversation with someone who is actively showing interest in and understanding what you are saying. You probably have a deeper conversation and connection with this person who leaves you feeling better about yourself. If you learn to apply this same consideration to others when they speak to you, you will generally leave with the same feelings of understanding and connectedness. Learn to really focus and interpret what others say to you. Listen to hear what they have to say, as opposed to listening to respond. Often, this is all most people are looking for and it is something you can do without much practice or effort.

Even when you feel you fully understand and comprehend the effect your emotions have in your life, there is still a component you may not be able to gain full control over. Negative thoughts can be terribly discouraging. These thoughts have often developed and have been strengthened through years of negative self-talk. When you have such a strong connection with the negative dialogue in your mind, even though you try desperately to eliminate it, you can feel as if you are just not meant to be happy. These thoughts are what can greatly hinder your ability to fully control your emotions.

Thank you so much for reading book I hope you have learned something.

CPSIA information can be obtained
at www.ICGtesting.com
Printed in the USA
LVHW011015140121
676458LV00010B/283